Victoria and Albert loved Scotland and built a holiday home at Balmoral. Albert also built a new home at Osborne in the Isle of Wight. Albert was very interested in art, science and manufacturing, and took a keen interest in the building of the Crystal Palace, an enormous building of glass and steel made for the Great Exhibition in 1851.

Albert died suddenly of typhoid in 1861. Victoria was overcome with grief. In her diary she wrote, 'My life as a happy person is ended!' She wore black for the rest of her life. For a long time she refused to appear in public.

This made her unpopular for a time. However she gradually began to enjoy life again. She was interested in the many new inventions such as the telephone and gramophone, and travelled about Britain on the railway.

In 1887 Victoria had been queen for 50 years and a great jubilee was held for her. She drove through the streets of London, cheered by thousands of people. As well as being queen, Victoria was head of a great Empire of different nations and her Diamond Jubilee was celebrated in the whole Empire.

Victoria died at the age of 80 on 22 January 1901, bringing the Victorian age to an end.

▲ *Victoria in old age surrounded by her children and grandchildren.*

▼ *The coronation of the young Queen.*

▲ *The wedding of Victoria and Albert.*

◀ *Queen Victoria, aged about 27.*

STEAM AND STEEL

The Victorian period was a time of great industrial change.

Before the reign of Queen Victoria, most spinning and weaving had been done by hand in country cottages. Then new machines were invented which used water power to turn the wheels of spinning machines. Huge factories were built to house these machines and many people moved from the country to the towns to work in them.

When James Watt built his steam engine, factory owners began to use steam power to turn their machines. Coal was needed as fuel for the steam engines, so more and more people were needed in the coal mines. At first, men and women carried sacks of coal up ladders from the coal face to the surface. Later on coal was lifted by winding gear powered by another Watt engine. Canals were built all over Britain to carry huge quantities of coal from the mines to the mills and factories.

Iron manufacturers used Watt's steam engines to crush iron ore dug from the soil. Iron was needed for hundreds of different products, such as bridges, saucepans and ploughs. In 1856 Henry Bessemer invented a way to make cheap steel from iron. His workmen produced steel goods for industry, for the new railways, for factories and the shipbuilding industry.

▼ *George Stephenson's locomotive 'The Rocket'.*

▼ *The steam hammer, developed in 1842, was used to beat large bits of metal into shape.*

▶ *Victorian miner's shovel. The handle could also be used as a hammer and a pick.*

▶ *A Victorian miner's lamp.*

In 1825 the first stretch of railway to carry both passengers and freight was opened between Stockton and Darlington. A huge crowd of people watched George Stephenson drive his railway engine *Locomotion* along the track. In 1829 a competition was held to find the best locomotive. Stephenson's *Rocket* reached a speed of 46 kilometres an hour and won the prize. During the 1830s and 1840s many other railways were opened.

The coming of the railways changed the lives of everybody in Britain. Passengers and goods could now be taken quickly and easily to all parts of the country. Coal and raw materials could be taken by rail to the factories, and the finished goods carried by rail to the towns and cities. Merchants also sent goods abroad in huge steam-powered ships made of steel.

The Great Exhibition of 1851 was a celebration of British industry. Manufacturers of china, pottery, furniture, ironware, clothing and household objects all displayed their goods. After the exhibition Britain was called the 'Workshop of the World'.

This period of change from making things by hand to making things in factories using machines is called the Industrial Revolution.

Fascinating Facts

In their early days canals were often called 'navigations' and the men who dug them were called 'navigators'. This was later shortened to 'navvy'. Railway navvies built the cuttings and embankments needed for the new railway lines.

▲ **The Crystal Palace, a huge iron and glass structure, was built specially for the Great Exhibition of 1851. There visitors could see displays of a wide range of manufactured goods.**

▼ **Work in the new factories was often low paid and unpleasant. Children as young as eight worked long hours in dangerous conditions.**

MEREDITH & DREW LTD.

Works:- Shadwell, London. E.
Our vans deliver daily in all parts of London & Suburbs

VICTORIANS AT HOME

The Industrial Revolution brought great changes to the way people lived.

At the beginning of Victoria's reign, most people lived in the country. Their cottages were small, damp, draughty and in bad repair. As industry moved from the country to towns, factory owners built crowded rows of cheap terrace houses for their workers. These soon turned into slums. The houses had no running water, no inside toilets or proper drains and no gardens. Water came from a tap or pump in the street, or was carried in buckets from nearby rivers. There was very little furniture, and the houses were lit by candles or oil lamps.

Factory workers spent long hours working for low wages, and many families could hardly afford to buy basic food and clothing. Women often took in washing and sewing to earn extra money, and even young children were sent out to work.

▲ *In the early years of Victoria's reign, many people still lived in humble one-roomed cottages.*

▼ *There was little fresh air or daylight between the tall, close-built houses in towns.*

Victorians had large families and ten children or more were quite normal.

The families of factory owners and members of the middle-class such as doctors, lawyers, bankers and businessmen lived much more comfortable lives. Their homes were in pleasant terraces, villas in the suburbs, or large mansions in the country. They often had several servants to look after them. In many towns and cities today you can still see these large middle-class homes. Many of them have now been divided into flats or offices.

On the ground floor, a middle-class Victorian home had a parlour or drawing-room, a dining-room, a large kitchen, a larder and the scullery where the washing-up was done. The bedrooms and nursery were on the first floor. Servants lived in cramped attic rooms. The main rooms were crowded with furniture, wax flowers, pictures, ornaments and photographs. In the 1870s gas lights replaced oil lamps in the homes of the wealthy, and by 1881 a few houses even had electric lights. Most of these houses had an indoor toilet, and servants carried jugs of hot water from the kitchen to fill up baths in front of the bedroom fire, or basins on the washstand.

◀ **Back-to-back houses in a Yorkshire town.**

▶ **Reconstructed middle-class Victorian drawing room in York's Castle Museum.**

In a middle-class family, only the father went out to work. Mothers stayed at home with the children and managed the household. Children were often cared for by a nanny and were expected to respect their elders, be quiet and obedient. A favourite Victorian saying was, 'Children should be seen and not heard'. When they grew up, girls were expected to learn to sing, sew, and play the piano so that later they would attract the attention of a suitable husband.

7

THE CLOTHES SHOW

Just as today, the amount Victorian people spent on clothes depended upon how well off they were.

Poorer people in Victorian Britain had to make their clothes last a long time. The smoke and dirt of factory life made it difficult to keep clothes clean. Working clothes were usually made of coarsely woven homespun cloth, or were bought from second-hand clothes shops. Children wore cast-offs from their parents or older children, and many had no shoes. But most people tried to keep a set of clothes for 'Sunday best'.

Wealthier families could afford better quality material and elegant dresses. Victorian ladies were often interested in fashion and read the fashion magazines to find out the latest styles.

The invention of a practical sewing machine by Isaac Merrit Singer in 1851 led to the mass production of clothing. This in turn changed the way people dressed.

Early Victorians wore wide skirts with flounces held out by crinolines, small bonnets were worn on their heads. Until 1900 narrow waists were fashionable. Ladies wore tightly-laced corsets, which restricted their breathing. Hairstyles became more elaborate with false pieces and fringes, while hats were designed for decoration rather than to cover the head.

Many ladies were so tightly laced that they would often faint. Some wore a bottle of smelling salts on a chain around their waists to revive them!

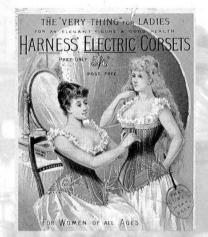

THE "VERY THING" FOR LADIES
FOR AN ELEGANT FIGURE & GOOD HEALTH
HARNESS' ELECTRIC CORSETS
PRICE ONLY 5/6
POST FREE
FOR WOMEN OF ALL AGES

▼ *By the 1870s the fashion had changed. Skirts were now draped over bustles. These were padded cushions tied behind the waist under the dress to make it stick out.*

► *The crinoline was the height of fashion in the early 1860s.*

Fascinating Facts

In Victorian times legs were never mentioned and were always covered up. Victorians even covered up the legs of their pianos!

Children of well-off families were dressed in very formal clothes.

Boys wore petticoats until the age of about six. Then they were dressed in sailor suits, or in velvet suits with lace collars and cuffs. They wore their hair in long curls.

Little girls wore shorter dresser than those of adult women, but the waists were nearly as tight.

The large background picture, Derby Day *by William Frith, shows a variety of clothes worn by Victorians.*

Well-off men wore knee-length frock-coats in silk or velvet, in plain, dark colours. They had silk waistcoats and wore a sash around the middle. Their shirts had stiff, high collars with cravats or ties around the neck.

Trousers at this time had no creases at the front, but were fastened by a strap under the shoes.

Beards and side whiskers were very fashionable, and men carried canes or walking sticks in their gloved hands.

Underneath, men wore long-sleeved woollen vests and long woollen underpants, which were often itchy and uncomfortable.

POVERTY AND CRIME

As towns grew in size, poverty increased and many people turned to a life of crime.

In 1801 only 20 per cent of the British population lived in towns. By 1901 it had risen to 75 per cent. London was the largest city, but other towns also grew rapidly as more and more people went there to find jobs in the new factories and industries.

Workers' houses were built in the centre of the towns, close to the factories. The houses were overcrowded, and sometimes six or seven people had to share a single bed. Many families lived in one room and took in a lodger to help with the rent. Cheap lodging houses in every city took in 20 or 30 people who slept on the floor with up to 12 in a single room.

City streets were filthy as there were no proper sewers or drains, and the air was polluted with smoke from the factory chimneys. Wealthier people could live in pleasant suburbs on the edge of the towns and travel in to work on the new railways.

▶ *Early policemen.*

The poverty in the city centres was so bad that many people turned to crime. House-breaking, theft and assault were common. Pickpockets, swindlers and forgers mingled with the crowds on the streets. Criminals were not often caught until Sir Robert Peel founded the Metropolitan Police of London. By 1839 police forces were being organised all over the country.

▼ *These barefoot children were photographed in London.*

Criminals were severely punished. Men and women could be flogged or sent to prison. Some convicts were sent to Australia, and others were sentenced to death by hanging.

Early Victorian jails were crowded and dirty. Prisoners were so badly fed that in one prison they are said to have eaten live worms and frogs. In another they melted candles into their soup to make it more nourishing.

Many women prisoners had their children in prison with them, where they lived under terrible conditions. Elizabeth Fry visited Newgate Prison and saw how overcrowded, dirty and unhealthy the prison was. She set up a school for the children and trained the women so they could get jobs when they were released.

Prisons were improved later in Victoria's reign. New prisons were built after 1840, and convicts were each given a clean cell where they lived alone. Prisoners had to remain silent all the time, even when they were eating, working or taking exercise.

▲ **Many prisoners died in the convict ships on the way to Australia.**

▼ **The poor lived in slums in the centre of Victorian cities.**

▲ **Prisoners had to walk a treadmill or turning staircase to get some exercise, but they were not allowed to speak to each other.**

Fascinating Facts

In 1830 there was a single farmhouse near the banks of the River Tees. By 1880, a new town called Middlesbrough had grown there with a population of 50,000 people.

WORKING WOMEN AND CHILDREN

Victorian working-class men were paid such low wages that women and children were also forced to work very long hours.

In some places children as young as five worked in the coal mines. The underground passages were sometimes too small for an adult to squeeze through, so children were harnessed to coal tubs which they dragged through the darkness on all fours. Some children worked the pumps, standing ankle deep in cold water for 12 hours at a stretch. Others worked alone in the dark, opening and shutting the doors to let the coal tubs through.

In the homes of the wealthy, climbing boys were forced to sweep chimneys. Many suffocated in the narrow, soot-filled chimneys. If a boy refused to climb up a chimney, a cruel boss might light a fire beneath him.

In country areas, women and children worked in small industries such as lace-making, straw-plaiting and glue-making. Workers were paid very low rates for the completed articles. Dressmakers worked 17 hours a day in cramped rooms with up to 12 other women and slept under their work tables.

▶ In 1888 the 'match girls' went on strike for better working conditions. Led by Annie Besant, they marched to the House of Commons and as a result won the strike.

◀ Crossing sweepers and match-sellers were among the lowest paid workers.

A report in the 1860s showed that 1,000 children worked as long as 16 hours a day. Half of all workers in the textile mills were under 18. Those who fell asleep at the looms were beaten. There were many terrible accidents in the factories because the machines were unguarded. Children lost arms, or grew up crippled after working long hours bent over their work.

RICH AND POOR

On the left is a poor child's rattle which was used for scaring crows on a farm. The silver toy rattle on the right would have belonged to a child from a richer family.

◀ *This romantic scene says little about the harsh reality of female factory workers' lives.*

One way to escape poverty was to become a domestic servant. If a young girl could get a job as a kitchen maid, although her wages might be low, she was fed and clothed. She might be promoted to parlour maid or cook. Boys hoped to leave the scullery or kitchen and become a footman or butler.

During the Victorian period, women of all classes were seen as the property of either their father or husband. Until 1870, all a wife's earnings belonged to her husband. Until 1882, all property belonged to the husband. Until 1891 a man could imprison his wife in their home. Children belonged to the husband.

▲ *Large families had a team of servants to look after them.*

Towards the end of the 19th century women began to fight for freedom, and women's suffrage societies, which fought for the female vote, were set up.

❝ *I have a belt round my waist, and a chain passing between my legs, and I go on my hands and feet. The road is very steep, and we have to hold on by a rope . . . it is very hard work for a woman.* ❞

Betty Harris, a pit worker

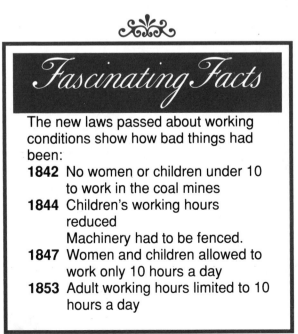

Fascinating Facts

The new laws passed about working conditions show how bad things had been:

1842 No women or children under 10 to work in the coal mines

1844 Children's working hours reduced
Machinery had to be fenced.

1847 Women and children allowed to work only 10 hours a day

1853 Adult working hours limited to 10 hours a day

13

RELIGION AND REFORM

Religion played an important part in the life of many Victorians.

In 1851, six out of ten people went to church every Sunday. Many new churches were built in the growing towns and cities, and old churches were restored. Baptisms, weddings and funerals were important social events. Most families held weekday prayers and said grace at every meal.

For most Victorians, Sunday was the only day they were not at work. It was usually spent resting and recovering from their weekly labours. Middle-class Victorians were very strict about how they spent the 'Lord's Day'. Children were not allowed to play with toys and were only allowed to read the Bible. Even very young children had to put away their toys, sit quietly and do nothing.

The whole family, including the servants, went to church, and the family sat in their own pew. The sermons were very long, and charity was a favourite subject. Enormous sums were raised to help the poor, but these were often wasted. In 1853 Parliament appointed Charity Commissioners to make sure the money given to charity was spent sensibly.

A group of Christians, known as the Evangelists, believed that the Church should be more interested in the sufferings of the poor.

Lord Shaftesbury was an Evangelist who helped to pass laws to improve life for workers in mines and factories. These laws meant that children no longer worked in the textile mills, women and children stopped working in coal mines, and boys no longer climbed chimneys. Shaftesbury also helped to reduce the working hours in factories, to start 'ragged schools' for poor children and to run soup kitchens for the hungry.

▶ *A wealthy lady and her daughter visit a sick village child in 1860.*

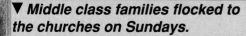
▼ *Middle class families flocked to the churches on Sundays.*

Shaftesbury encouraged Thomas Barnardo in his work among the homeless boys of London. In 1870 Dr Barnardo opened his first home which took in poor boys and gave them food and shelter. Later on he opened other homes in different parts of the country for both boys and girls.

In 1878 William Booth created the Salvation Army, which provided night shelters, hostels and soup kitchens for the poor. At first people laughed at the Army, and its members were fined and imprisoned for causing a nuisance. But Booth kept on with his work and people eventually came to respect him.

▼ *A Salvation Army hostel in London.*

► *The Victorians were fond of religious and moral poems and texts which they hung on their walls.*

THE HAPPY HOME.

Happy the home, when God is there,
And love fills every breast;
Where one their wish, and one their prayer,
And one their heavenly rest.

Happy the home where Jesus' name
Is sweet to every ear;
Where children early lisp His fame,
And parents hold Him dear.

Happy the home where prayer is heard,
And praise is wont to rise;
Where parents love the sacred Word,
And live but for the skies.

Lord, let us in our homes agree,
This blessed peace to gain;
Unite our hearts in love to Thee,
And love to all will reign.

GOING TO SCHOOL

As laws were passed to reduce children's working hours, more and more children started going to school.

At the beginning of Victoria's reign, many wealthier people thought that education would make the working-class discontented with their lives. Only the church or charitable organisations provided children with some education in dame schools, Sunday schools or charity schools.

Dame schools, run by women in their own houses, taught arithmetic, reading and writing. Sunday schools and charity schools taught reading and Bible stories. A few rich factory owners, like Robert Owen in Lanarkshire and Sir Titus Salt in Yorkshire, set up schools in their factories for their child workers. But most children had no chance to go to school at all. They went to work in the mines and factories at the age of six or seven and were too tired to go to school when they were not working. In London in 1840, Ragged Schools were set up to educate homeless children and orphans and teach them a useful trade. They were called 'Ragged' because so many of the pupils wore rags.

When children's working hours were reduced in 1844, more children began to go to school for half a day. The teacher taught the older pupils, called monitors, and the monitors in turn taught the younger children. Children learned their lessons by heart and chanted their tables and answers in chorus. Classes were very large and the teacher often beat the children to make them behave.

▼ *A botany class at a London school for girls.*

$$6 \times 8 = 48$$
$$7 \times 8 = 56$$

Fascinating Facts

Children practised their writing and arithmetic by writing on slates with chalk. When the slate was full, the pupil could wipe it clean and re-use it.

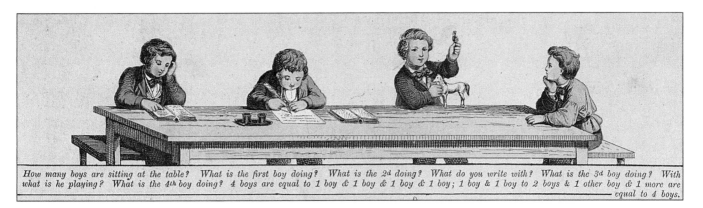

How many boys are sitting at the table? What is the first boy doing? What is the 2d doing? What do you write with? What is the 3d boy doing? With what is he playing? What is the 4th boy doing? 4 boys are equal to 1 boy & 1 boy & 1 boy & 1 boy; 1 boy & 1 boy to 2 boys & 1 other boy & 1 more are equal to 4 boys.

▲ *An extract from a Victorian school book.*

In 1870 Parliament passed an Education Act which said that all children between the ages of five and ten should go to school. School Boards or committees were set up and many new schools were built – some are still used as schools today.

Parents paid a few pence each week to send their children to these Board Schools. But the poorest parents could not afford to pay and kept their children away from school. Even in 1891, when Board Schools became free, many parents did not send their children because they needed the money the children were earning. Factory owners didn't want to lose their low-paid child workers, so the School Boards agreed that children could work in the factory before school and after finishing at school, until 10 p.m.

Middle-class parents paid for their children to go to schools. Anybody who wanted could set up a boarding school. Children were often badly taught and sometimes treated cruelly. At Bowes Academy in Yorkshire, 25 pupils died between 1810 and 1834 of starvation, disease or neglect.

Wealthy young children were taught at home by tutors or governesses. At the age of seven, boys went to one of the public schools like Rugby, Winchester, Eton and Harrow. The main aim of these schools was to study Latin and Greek grammar. These schools were known for the amount of bullying, drinking and gambling among the pupils.

▼ *Rugby School in 1841.*

HEALTH AND MEDICINE

As more and more people moved into the towns, they became filthy, polluted places.

The large amount of people in towns produced a lot of waste, but there was no proper system for getting rid of it. Sewage was emptied into the same rivers and streams that people used for their drinking water. This led to the rapid spread of diseases such as cholera, typhus and typhoid. Poor housing conditions, with dirty and airless rooms, meant that many people died from consumption or tuberculosis.

In 1842 Edwin Chadwick produced a report that showed the link between poor living conditions and public health. However, it was only when a bad outbreak of cholera occurred in 1848 that people began to take any notice. In 1855 engineers built the Embankment beside the Thames in London. Buried in the Embankment was a wide pipe which took most of London's sewage down river before allowing it to flow out into the Thames. But it was not until 1875 that Parliament passed a law to provide clean water supplies and good drainage in towns, and gave councils the power to clear away slum houses.

▼ *Building a modern sewage system for London, 1862.*

▲ *Surgical instruments.*

Fascinating Facts

Londoners called 1858 'The Year of the Great Stink' because of the foul smell that came from the mud flats of the River Thames at low tide. It was so bad that Members of Parliament had to stop their discussions, and people crossing the bridge felt sick.

At the beginning of Victoria's reign, doctors knew very little about the cause of diseases and how to cure them. Surgical operations were carried out without pain-killers, and many patients died of shock. It was not until James Simpson used chloroform successfully that patients could hope for a painless operation.

Medicine made great advances after 1856 when in France Louis Pasteur proved that small living organisms called bacteria, or germs, caused disease. Joseph Lister realised that germs were responsible for the infection of wounds. In 1867 he invented an antiseptic spray to kill germs. As a result, operations became much safer.

At that time, nurses were on the same level as servants, and nursing was not a job for respectable women. Despite this, Florence Nightingale was determined to work with the sick. In 1854 she took a party of nurses to look after wounded British soldiers in Turkey. Florence worked 20 hours a day to prevent soldiers dying from fever and infection. She became a national heroine, and on her return to Britain she was given £45,000. She used this money to start the Nightingale Training School for Nurses at St Thomas's Hospital in London.

▲ This cartoon shows how the filthy waters of the river Thames caused disease.

▼ Medical discoveries greatly improved dentistry.

Mary Seacole (1805-1881)

Mary Seacole was born in Jamaica in the West Indies, where she learned how to look after sick people from her mother.

When Mary heard about the war in the Crimea, she decided to join Florence Nightingale. Mary travelled to England and asked permission to go to Scutari, but was turned down because she was black. Mary then decided to take a boat to the Crimea at her own expense. Once there she built a store and a kitchen near the front lines. Every day she took food and medicine to where the fighting was the fiercest.

When the war ended, Mary went back to London and was cheered in the streets. She later wrote a book about her adventures in the Crimea, which was a great success.

SHOPS AND SERVICES

Many people opened shops and started businesses to provide goods and services for the growing populations of Victorian towns.

In any city street you might find a shoe-maker, an ironmonger, a barber, a tailor, a grocer or a chemist. Street traders also sold all sorts of goods, and all day the streets were noisy with their cries: *'Lovely sweet violets,'* *'Muffins for sale'* or *'Milko – a penny a pint'.*

▲ *Examples of early food packaging.*

◀ *People bought some foodstuffs loose and put them into their own containers, like this spice turret, at home.*

▲ *A London barrow boy.*

At first each shopkeeper sold only one kind of goods. Every morning fruit, flowers and vegetables were sent from the country to Covent Garden market in London. Greengrocers went to the market early in the morning to buy fresh produce for their own shops. Fishmongers bought their supplies from Billingsgate fish market. Sheep and cattle were driven through the streets to be slaughtered at Smithfield or Islington, where their meat was sold to butchers.

In poor districts, street traders sold cooked food and drinks. Bread was sold in the streets for a penny a loaf. At a soup house, for twopence or threepence you could buy a basin of soup, potatoes and a slice of bread. Coffee stalls sold coffee, tea and cocoa at a penny a mug, as well as ham sandwiches, boiled eggs, baked potatoes and slices of cake or bread and butter.

▼ *The book department at a big department store*

Fascinating Facts

Grocery shops sold goods 'loose' and each item had to be separately weighed and wrapped for each customer. Liquids were measured into jugs brought by the customer.

▲ *Flower girls were a common sight.*

▼ *A Victorian grocery shop.*

Chop houses provided a good lunch for those with a little more money. One shilling and sixpence would buy a plate of liver and bacon, bread and potatoes, cheese and celery, and a pint of stout.

In 1844, a group of weavers in Rochdale, Lancashire opened the first co-operative grocery shop. Co-operatives soon became popular because the people who ran them shared their profits with their customers. Later on, in 1876, Thomas Lipton started a chain of grocery stores in Scotland.

By the end of Victoria's reign, tinned foods became available and this gave people much more choice in what they ate. Fewer goods were now sold in the streets and more in the shops. People could also buy goods from the new department stores that opened in the large cities.

In the country, men travelled from place to place selling goods, mending broken objects or providing entertainment. Towards the end of the Victorian period these people became less common as village shops started to provide what country people needed.

21

TRAVEL AND TRANSPORT

The coming of the railways meant that people who had never travelled further than the next village could now travel more widely.

Fares were cheap and day trips to seaside resorts like Brighton, Great Yarmouth, Margate and Blackpool were very popular. These towns doubled in size within a few years.

▶ *A Victorian railway lamp.*

▲ *The railway revolutionised travel.*

In 1860 the first horse-drawn trams appeared. They ran on small rails sunk into the road and were instantly popular. In 1885 electric trams, with overhead wires, began to replace the horse-drawn trams.

Victorian railways were divided into different classes of travel. Wealthy passengers travelled in comfortable, closed-in first class carriages with padded seats. Second class carriages had wooden seats and open sides. Third class passengers had no seats and no roofs over their head to protect them from the weather, smoke and fumes. In 1846 a law was passed that all railway carriages should be roofed.

In towns, people travelled in horse-drawn buses. Those who could afford it hired a hansom cab, an enclosed horse-drawn vehicle. The wealthy had their own large coaches.

At the time that George Stevenson was developing a steam locomotive for railways, Sir Goldsworthy Gurney was developing a steam road carriage which could carry 18 passengers. In 1865 a law was passed which limited the speed of road steamers to six kilometres an hour. A person had to walk in front of the steamer holding a red flag by day, or a red lamp at night.

▶ *A London horse-drawn bus.*

In 1865 a new form of transport, the petrol driven 'horseless carriage', caught the attention of the rich. These cars were all made by hand so only the very wealthy could afford to buy them.

London was the first town in the world to have an underground railway. It opened in 1863, and grew rapidly as new lines were built to link the business districts with the suburbs.

As the roads improved during Victoria's reign, cycling became a popular sport. The early bicycles, called 'penny-farthings', had a big front wheel and a small back wheel and were uncomfortable and difficult to ride. In 1885 'safety bicycles' were introduced where both the wheels were the same size and connected to the pedals by a chain drive.

▼ Early cars had nothing to protect the passengers from the weather.

Fascinating Facts

At first cycling was a sport for men, because the Victorians did not think it was 'ladylike!' In the late 1890s women also began to ride bicycles, in spite of their long skirts.

▲ In the 1890s everyone who could afford one owned a bike, and parks and country lanes were crowded with cyclists on Saturdays and holidays.

TRADE AND EMPIRE

During the Victorian period, the British Empire was one of the biggest in the world.

An empire is a group of countries ruled by one person or government. By 1900 Queen Victoria ruled over nearly a quarter of all the people in the world.

Many British people worked in these foreign countries, for the government or the army, or as merchants and traders. Victorian missionaries went out to teach the native people the Christian way of life. Most Victorians believed that the Empire was good for the people they ruled over. But few of them understood the different cultures of the local people.

▲ *Stamps from different parts of Victoria's empire.*

▼ *Victorian Jubilee plate of 1887, showing the Empire and imports and exports.*

The British Empire developed gradually from the new colonies where, from 1600 onwards, settlers from Britain had gone to make a new life. Trading companies were set up to develop trade with the colonies in America, Canada, the West Indies, West Africa and India.

The Victorians wanted to increase their trade and their control over more countries. Hong Kong island was seized from the Chinese in 1841. From 1880 on a great 'scramble for Africa' took place as European nations divided up the continent among themselves. In 1882 the British conquered Egypt, and soon occupied much of East and Central Africa.

◀ *The image of Britannia, used to represent the power of the Empire, is still used today.*

From 1815 onwards hundreds of thousands of people left Britain to settle in Canada, Australia, New Zealand and South Africa. The people who were already living there lost most of their land to the white settlers.

Many countries disliked being ruled by Britain. Thirteen American colonies had already won their independence from British rule to become the United States of America. Between 1843 and 1872 the Maori people in New Zealand fought the British for control of their land. A rebellion by the Jamaicans in 1865 was put down with great brutality. In South Africa, the British suffered a defeat by the native Zulu people in 1880.

▲ The British often treated the natives of colonies brutally. Here, Britannia portrays the power and authority of the British over the natives during the Zulu War.

▼ Launched in 1869, The Cutty Sark is the only survivor of the British tea-clippers that carried tea from China to Britain.

The Boers, the Dutch settlers who had arrived in South Africa before the British, tried to stop the British gaining control of the gold mines, and declared war on the British in 1899. This was the Boer War.

In India there was continual fighting between the Indian princes and the British rulers. In 1857 Indian troops rose up in a great mutiny against their British officers, but the British army was too strong and the Indians were defeated. Afterwards many more parts of India were brought under British control.

In 1876, Queen Victoria was proclaimed Empress of India at a great ceremony at Delhi.

▶ Until Victorian times, tea was a luxury few people could afford. During the 19th century, tea was imported from India as well as China and Sri Lanka (Ceylon), and soon became a popular everyday drink.

25

THE IRISH QUESTION

When Victoria came to the throne, she became Queen of the United Kingom of Great Britain and Ireland.

In 1801 the Act of Union had been passed, which put the Irish people under the rule of Parliament in London.

Most Irish people were Roman Catholics. Irish Catholics had only been given the right to vote and to own land in 1829, and many were unhappy about the way they had been treated. The land on which they lived was owned by English landlords, who used an agent to collect the rents. These tenant farmers were very poor and lived in fear of losing their homes. The Protestants living in Ulster (Northern Ireland) were better off. Their land was more fertile, and new textile factories and the shipbuilding industry brought wealth to the city of Belfast.

By 1840 there were well over 8 million people in Ireland. Most lived mainly on potatoes which they grew in the fields around their small houses. In 1845 a plant disease, the potato blight, spoiled the potato crop. The next two years brought terrible famine. About 1.3 million people died of starvation, and of the famine fever that followed it. A further 1.4 million left Ireland. Most went to the United States, some went to Britain, and others to Australia and Canada. People continued to emigrate from Ireland for the next 100 years.

▼ A 'loy', used for planting potatoes.

The inside of an Irish peasant's hut during the famine of 1845-49.

▼ The village of Tullig was abandoned after the famine.

Many Irish people blamed Britain for doing so little to help. A large group, led by Charles Stuart Parnell, wanted 'Home Rule' for Ireland, that is an Irish parliament to look after Irish affairs. Parnell also supported the Irish farmers who refused to pay their rent. In 1881 he was put in prison. A period of violence followed in Ireland.

❛I shall never forget the change in one week in August. On the first occasion, on an official visit of inspection, I had passed over 32 miles, thickly studded with potato fields in bloom. The next time the face of the whole country was changed; the stalk remained bright green but the leaves were all scorched black. It was the work of a night.❜

From a description of the potato famine by a government official, 1846

Fascinating Facts

Ulster Protestants feared that Home Rule would mean 'Rome rule' that is rule by the Roman Catholic Church.

▼ *Charles Stewart Parnell, who led the movement for Home Rule.*

Rents were not paid, and families were forced out of their homes. The British government had to agree to free Parnell and help the farmers to pay off their debts and buy their own land.

By 1885 Home Rule had become so popular in Ireland that Parnell's Party had 86 Members of Parliament. The Prime Minister, William Gladstone, needed Parnell's help to stay in power and so he decided to grant Home Rule to Ireland. However, most members of Parliament wanted to keep the Act of Union, and so they voted against the Bills in 1886 and 1893. The Irish problem remained unsettled.

INVENTIONS AND DISCOVERIES

There were many inventions and discoveries during Victoria's reign which changed the way everyone lived.

The invention of the telegraph meant that messages could be sent over long distances by passing electric signals along a wire. The first public telegram service started in 1843. Messages sent by telegraph were written out on telegram forms and delivered by a messenger.

The telephone, invented in 1875 by Alexander Graham Bell, was slow to catch on at first because it was so expensive. Women sat in front of switchboards of exchanges to connect up the calls of the earliest telephones.

In 1877 Thomas Edison, who had invented the first electric light bulbs, invented the phonograph or gramophone. He recorded his own voice reciting *Mary had a little lamb*. The phonograph had a handle to wind up the clockwork motor which turned the record round and round.

Telephones and typewriters made a great difference in Victorian offices. The first typewriters to go on sale were made by the Remington company in the United States in 1874. Isaac Pitman had already invented shorthand, a way of writing as quickly as a person can dictate. Many women now began to work in offices as secretaries.

▼ *The phonograph or 'wonderful talking machine' was the latest thing in popular entertainment.*

◀ *To make a call on a Victorian telephone you spoke into a mouthpiece and asked to be connected through the exchange.*

▲ *The Great Britain.*

◀ *Advertisement for typewriters.*

Early cars and bicycles had solid rubber tyres, but the invention of the air-filled pneumatic tyre made road travel much more comfortable.

At sea, sailing ships were replaced by ships with steam engines which turned screw propellers. In 1843 Isambard Kingdom Brunel launched the *Great Britain*, the first all-iron ship with a screw propeller to cross the Atlantic.

In Victorian kitchens, the main problem in the summer was to keep food fresh. The development of tinned and bottled goods meant that food could be stored for longer. By 1855 tinned meat, dried milk, and ready-packaged goods with 'brand names' were sold in the shops.

When gas was piped to the homes of the wealthy, gas fires and gas cookers went on the market, and gas lamps replaced candles and oil lamps. Housework was made easier by the invention of a hand operated washing-machine, and of a carpet sweeper which had revolving brushes to pick up the dirt. By the end of the century clothes were made on a sewing machine.

The Victorians were fascinated by cameras and took many photographs. The people being photographed had to keep very still because it took a long time to produce a picture.

◀ *Patience was required to have your photograph taken by an early camera.*

BOOKS AND WRITERS

When Victoria came to the throne, the only books for children were tales full of dreadful punishments for bad or disobedient children.

In 1823 *Grimm's Fairy Tales* were translated into English and later on Hans Christian Anderson's stories were also translated. But most writers still believed that when children read a book, they must learn something from it.

In 1863 Charles Kingsley's classic children's book *The Water Babies* was published. This expressed Kingsley's concerns about the sufferings of working children.

◀ *Long John Silver, from Robert Louis Stevenson's first full length novel* Treasure Island, *which brought him fame and fortune.*

The first book to be published with the aim of entertaining children, rather than improving them, was *Alice's Adventures in Wonderland* (1865) by Lewis Carroll. After this, other authors began to write stories about ordinary children. There were tales of adventure like Robert Louis Stevenson's *Treasure Island*, and stories about animals like Anna Sewell's *Black Beauty*. Rudyard Kipling wrote the *Just So Stories* to amuse children, and Edward Lear's *Book of Nonsense* was an immediate success. Some of these old books are so good that they are still popular today.

◀ *A page from* Alice's Adventures in Wonderland, *written by Lewis Carroll.*

Charles Dickens (1812-1870)

We know a lot about what life was like in Victorian times from the writings of Charles Dickens. Dickens wrote vividly about the lives of ordinary people. His first novel *Oliver Twist* attacked the way poor orphans were treated. *Nicholas Nickleby* describes cruel boarding schools so well that many were forced to close down following such bad publicity.

▲ *Novels written by the Brontë sisters, Anne, Emily and Charlotte include* Jane Eyre *and* Wuthering Heights *which have become popular classics.*

▼ *In his novel* Bleak House, *published in 1853, Dickens described the hard life of Jo the crossing-sweeper.*

In the 1890s comics began to appear. The first Victorian comics were called 'penny dreadfuls'. They had few pictures and the story was told in words.

In 1850 public libraries were set up in every town so people were able to read books even if they could not afford to buy them.

◀ *Charles Dickens wrote his books using a quill pen.*

INDEX

Africa 24, 25
Albert, Prince 2-3
Australia 11, 25

Balmoral 3
Barnardo, Thomas 15
Bell, Alexander Graham 28
Besant, Annie 12
Bessemer, Henry 4
bicycles 23
Billingsgate 20
Board Schools 17
boarding schools 17
Booth, William 15
Brontë sisters 31
Brunel, Isambard Kingdom 29
buses 22
bustles 8

cameras 28-29
Canda 24, 25
canals 4
Caroll, Lewis 30
cars 22-23
Chadwick, Edwin 18
charity 14-15
chimney sweeps 12
chop house 21
church 14-15
clothes 8-9
co-operatives 21
coal mines 4, 12, 13
convicts 11
corset 8
Covent Garden 20
crime 10-11
Crimean War 19
crinolines 8
Crystal Palace 3, 5

dame schools 16
department stores 20, 21
Dickens, Charles 31
doctors 18-19
drains 18
Edison, Thomas 28
Education Act 17
Egypt 24
electricity 7, 29
Eliot, George 30
Empire 3, 24-25
Evangelists 14

factories 4-5, 6-7
famine 26-27

frock-coats 9
Fry, Elizabeth 11
furniture 7

gas 7, 29
gramophone 28
Great Exhibition 3, 5

Home Rule 26-27
Hong Kong 24
houses 6-7

India 24-25
Industrial Revolution 4-5
Ireland 26-27
iron 4

Jamaica 25

Kipling, Rudyard 30

Lear, Edward 30
libraries 31
Lister, Joseph 19

match girls 12
medicine 18-19
mines 4
missionaries 24

Nightingale, Florence 19
nurses 19

oil lamps 7, 29
Osborne 3
Owen, Robert 16

Parnell, Charles Stuart 27
Pasteur, Louis 19
Peel, Sir Robert 10
penny-farthings 23
phonograph 28
photographs 28, 29
Pitman, Isaac 28
police 10
potatoes 26
prison 11
public health 18-19
public schools 16-17

ragged schools 16
railways 5, 22-23
roads 22-23

Salt, Sir Titus 16
Salvation Army 15
schools 16-17
Seacole, Mary 19
servants 7, 13
Sewell, Anna 30
Shaftsbury, Lord 14-15
shipbuilding 29
slums 6
Smithfield 20
South Africa 25
steam power 4-5, 22-23
steel 4-5
Stephenson, George 5, 22
Stevenson, Robert Louis 30
suburbs 7
Sunday schools 16
sweated labour 12-13

telephone 28
terrace houses 6-7
textile mills 4
toilets 6
towns 6
trams 23
trousers 9
typewriter 28
typhoid 18

underground 23

Watt, James 4
West Indies 24
Wilberforce, William